LIFE'S JOURNEYS

BY
NADINE M. HUGMEYER

National Library of Canada Cataloguing in Publication Data

A cataloguing record for this book that includes the U.S. Library of Congress Classification number, the Library of Congress Call number and the Dewey Decimal cataloguing code is available from the National Library of Canada. The complete cataloguing record can be obtained from the National Library's online database at: www.nlc-bnc.ca/amicus/index-e.html

ISBN: 1-4120-3502-3

TRAFFORD

This book was published on-demand in cooperation with Trafford Publishing.
On-demand publishing is a unique process and service of making a book available for retail sale to the public taking advantage of on-demand manufacturing and Internet marketing. On-demand publishing includes promotions, retail sales, manufacturing, order fulfilment, accounting and collecting royalties on behalf of the author.

Suite 6E, 2333 Government St., Victoria, B.C. V8T 4P4, CANADA

Phone	250-383-6864	Toll-free 1-888-232-4444 (Canada & US)
Fax	250-383-6804	E-mail sales@trafford.com
Web site	www.trafford.com	TRAFFORD PUBLISHING IS A DIVISION OF TRAFFORD HOLDINGS LTD.
Trafford Catalogue #04-1330		www.trafford.com/robots/04-1330.html

PREFACE

As children we are molded by the decisions our parents make for us. As we grow and experiment with life, we begin to make our own choices in some attempt to break from that mold and discover who we are. We begin to choose our own paths with little knowledge that every heart we touch; every tear that falls and every stranger we come in contact with places us at a crossroad. We can either choose to continue on or go another way. Each choice can and will lead us to something new, whether it is overwhelming joy or heart wrenching sadness. Each path will be a journey in itself, a gift for us to learn from and hopefully grow because of.

With that being said, welcome to a few of life's journeys. The roads people took, the choices they made and the people that were affected are all here for you to see. Their paths have at one time or another come across mine and I felt for them. My hope is that you can feel what they went through and maybe even learn from them. Lord knows I did.

CONTENTS

I LOVE:

II LOST HOPE:

III FAMILIES:

IV NATURE:

BLESSED TEARS	05-30-91
WINTER	11-14-03
AUTUMN MORNINGS	11-27-03

V MISCELLANEOUS:

MY PRINCE	02-21-84
WHISPERS	02-20-85
PRINCE	03-26-85
ANGEL	05-17-85
HELL	05-17-85
SUMMER VACATION	05-22-85
SALEM	06-07-85
SPRING BREAK	10-08-85
FUTURES	12-08-86
DRAGONS	09-24-91
RAINBOWS	04-12-92
FREEDOM	04-19-92
DREAMS	05-31-92
RUN AWAY	02-13-93
RAPE IS	07-03-93
TRUST / TRAGEDY	07-04-93
TIME	07-06-93
KUTULU	09-10-93
DREAMS	10-08-93
CHARMS	11-16-93
ADAM & EVE	08-10-93
HOPES & DREAMS	09-09-94

V MISCELLANEOUS (cont'd)

DO IT	10-20-94
HALLOWEEN	10-31-03
CRYSTAL AXE	11-20-03
TIME	11-20-03

VI CARDS:

VALENTINE	02-12-87
VALENTINE	02-03-88
A CHRISTMAS WISH	11-25-89
CHRISTMAS	11-30-89
A BIRTHDAY WISH	02-05-90
THE ONE	07-27-92
VALENTINE	02-11-93
VALENTINE	02-11-93
VALENTINE	02-13-94
IT CAN'T BE CHRISTMAS	11-27-03

LOVE

LOVE...

LOVE IS
LIKE A ROSE IN
BLOOM FOREVER GROWING –
EACH DAY FULLER AND STRONGER THAN
BEFORE

HE...

HE IS
A GENTLE AND
LOVING PERSON WITH TRUE
SENSITIVITY AND I CARE
FOR HIM

NEVER...

NO, I NEVER MET YOU
AND I HAVEN'T CARED
I HAVEN'T EVEN LOVED YOU
YET, LOOK WHAT THINGS WE'VE SHARED
I HAVE NEVER TOUCHED YOU
SO TENDER LIKE I COULD
AND I HAVE NEVER KISSED YOU
AS SWEETLY AS I WOULD
I HAVE NEVER HELD YOU
SO DEEP WITHIN MY HEART
THAT WHEN EVER YOU'RE AWAY
I BEGIN TO FALL APART
I HAVE NEVER WHISPERED
SWEET NOTHINGS IN YOUR EAR
AND I HAVE NEVER WISHED FOR
A DAY WITH YOU RIGHT HERE
I HAVE NEVER DENIED
THAT THERE'S WORLD ABOVE
AND I NEVER THOUGHT FOR ONCE
I'D BE FALLING IN LOVE

ONCE ADORED...

FOREVER IS LONG
WHEN WE CHOOSE NOT TO SPEAK
OUR LIES BECOME DAGGERS
WHEN IT'S TRUTH THAT WE SEEK

OUR WORDS BECOME WEAPONS
OUR TONGUES ARE LIKE SWORDS
THEN HEARTS ARE TURNED COLD
TO THOSE ONCE ADORED

LOVE...

A LOT OF ANGER
A LITTLE HATE
YET ALL THE JOY
IS WORTH THE WAIT

TRUTH WITHIN...

TO WALK ALONG A GRASSY ROAD
AND SEE THE WORLD ANEW
TO BREATHE THE AIR OF PASSION
AND TO DREAM OF ONLY YOU
TO SEE THE FIRE WITHIN YOUR EYES
AND KNOW IT'S NOT A LIE
TO FEEL YOUR ARMS ABOUT MY WAIST
AND NOT TO QUESTION WHY
TO HOLD YOUR HEART WITHIN MY HANDS
AND TASTE YOUR SWEETENED SMILE
TO KNOW THE LOVE WAS OURS TO LIVE
IF EVEN FOR A WHILE
TO FEEL YOUR WARM CARESSES
AND DRY YOUR SORROWED TEARS
TO HOLD YOU VERY TIGHTLY
AND WISH AWAY YOUR FEARS
TO HAVE YOU KNOW, MY SOUL IS YOURS
UNTIL THE DAY WE DIE
TO FIND THE STRENGTH IN WEAKNESS
AND THE TRUTH WITHIN THE LIE

MY EYES...

HERE'S A WINDOW TO MY SOUL
LOOK AND SEE WHAT'S HERE
FIND THE ANSWERS IN MY EYES
AND FORGET YOUR DEEPEST FEARS
MY EYES COULD TELL YOU STORIES
OF JOY AND BITTER PAIN
THEY COULD SHARE THE MEMORIES
OF LOVE THAT WAS IN VAIN
THESE EYES COULD SHOW THE WAY I FELT
WHEN WE WERE TORN APART
THEY COULD PROVE THE TEARS THAT FELL
WITH THIS LONELY BROKEN HEART
THESE EYES WILL SAY I LOVE YOU
ALONG WITH MY HEART AND MIND
THESE EYES WILL SHOW YOU HONESTY
WHICH IN WORDS YOU'LL NEVER FIND

LOVE...

IT CAME
OVER ME LIKE
AN OCEAN FULL OF WAVES
UNTO THE SAND. ALL I COULD DO
WAS LOVE

CONFESSIONS...

I'VE DONE A LOT OF STUPID THINGS
AND SOME I CAN'T FORGET
I'VE SAID A LOT OF HATEFUL WORDS
TO THOSE THAT I HAVE MET
AND IN THE YEARS OF YESTERDAY
I'VE MADE MY SHARE OF FRIENDS
BUT IN THESE MOMENTS SOON TO PASS
A LOVE WILL REACH ITS END
WHEN I KNEW THE TRUTH WOULD HURT
I TOLD SOME BITTER LIES
THEN, IN THE HOURS WE LAY CLOSE
I HELD THEM WITH A SIGH
I KNOW OLD WOUNDS ARE MENDING
AND IT'S HARD TO RIGHT THE WRONG
I KNOW APOLOGIES ARE WORTHLESS
WHEN THEY'VE BEEN SAID FOR SO LONG
BUT NOW I HAVE A SECOND CHANCE
TO BUILD MY WORLD UPRIGHT
AND TELL YOU ALL THE SECRETS I HELD
IN YOUR ARMS EACH LONELY NIGHT

IN VAIN...

OUR THOUGHTS WERE ONCE ENTANGLED
NOW OUR HEARTS ARE IN MUCH PAIN
DAYS OF PLEASANT MEMORIES
A LOVE THAT'S NOT IN VAIN
THE HATEFUL WORDS OF ANGER
WERE SPOKE TO HIDE THE TEARS
A BITTER MISUNDERSTANDING
OF A LOVER'S BIGGEST FEAR
TO SAY WE LOVE IS SIMPLE
YET, IT'S HARD TO STAY AND FIGHT
AND TO GIVE AWAY A LOVE SO DEEP
IS A WRONG WE CANNOT RIGHT
THIS LOVE DOES CAUSE A YEARNING
MUCH DEEPER THAN IT SEEMS
A FIRE THAT BURNS WITHIN OUR SOUL
OF WHICH MOST CAN ONLY DREAM

MY HEART...

IF I GIVE YOU MY HEART
WOULD YOU TAKE IT FOR SURE
WITH NO QUESTIONS ASKED
WOULD YOU KEEP IT SAFE
AND HOLD IT TIGHT
OR RETURN IT, LIKE OTHERS PAST
AND WOULD YOU DARE
TO KEEP IT FOREVER
SAFE UNDER LOCK AND KEY
WOULD YOU BREAK IT UP
AND GIVE IT BACK
NOT RETURNING THE LOVE TO ME
COULD YOU GRANT ME
MY FONDEST DREAMS
NO MATTER WHAT THEY WERE
BRINGING ME HOPES
OF HAPPIER DAYS
AND A LOVE THAT WILL ENDURE

THROUGH THE ASHES...

I GAVE MY HEART
TO A GENTLE MAN
BACK A MILLION YEARS
HE TOOK IT FREELY
HELD IT TIGHT
AND KISSED AWAY MY FEARS
YET ALL THE LOVE
THAT HE DID GIVE
WAS NOT ENOUGH FOR ME
MY SOUL HALF HIS
STILL CRIED AT NIGHT
LONGING TO BE FREE
AND UNTO MYSELF
IN THAT SILENCE LAY
THAT SECRET STILL UNKNOWN
NOW UP THROUGH THOSE ASHES
OF THE LIES AND THE PAIN
A BRIGHTER DAY HAS SHOWN

TO MY LOVE...

WHAT SADNESS HOLDS
THY WEARY HEART
FRET NOT MY LOVE
THAT WE'RE APART
FOR ANY BOND
SO RARE AND TRUE
ENDS NOT WITH TIME
MY LOVE FOR YOU

LOVE...

LOVE IS
LIKE AN OCEAN
WAVE. YOU FOLLOW IT AND
CATCH IT. IT BRINGS YOU UP FAST AND
DOWN HARD

SPECIAL THINGS...

WHEN I SHUT MY EYES TO DREAM
ALL I SEE IS YOU
WHEN I CLOSED MY HEART TO LOVE
YOU CAME CRASHING THROUGH
WHEN I FEEL MY WORLD IS CRUMBLING
YOU'RE WHAT BRACES ME
WHEN I FEEL I'VE BEEN IMPRISONED
IT'S YOUR LOVE THAT SETS ME FREE
THERE'S SOMETHING IN THE WAY YOU SMILE
EACH AND EVERYDAY
SOMETHING IN THE WAY YOU LOVE
A LIGHT TO GUIDE THE WAY
THERE'S SOMETHING IN YOUR PRECIOUS EYES
AND THE WAY YOU LOOK AT ME
SOMETHING IN YOUR TENDER TOUCH
WHEN YOU'RE HOLDING ME
WITH ALL OF THE LITTLE THINGS
YOU'VE NEVER TRIED TO DO
WITH ALL THE WORDS YOU'VE SPOKEN
YOU'VE WARMED ME THROUGH AND THROUGH
I HAVE NOTHING AS GRAND TO GIVE
FOR EVERYTHING YOU'VE DONE
BUT IF IT'S ANY CONSEQUENCE
IT'S MY HEART THAT YOU HAVE WON

I AM – SHE...

I AM SHE
THAT HOLDS YOU CLOSE
DEEP WITHIN MY HEART
AND FEELS YOUR SORROW
AND YOUR JOY
EVEN WHEN APART
I AM SHE
THAT LOVES YOU MORE
THAN MOST WILL EVER KNOW
AND IF IT ALL BE SAID & DONE
IT'S I
WHO'D BID YOU GO

PURE LOVE...

WHEN YOU FIND THE PERFECT MATE
YOUR SOULS BECOME AS ONE
AND ANY PROBLEMS YE TWO SHALL FACE
WILL BE A BATTLE WON
IN THE EYES OF MOST MANKIND
YOU'LL SEE A JEALOUS HEART
FOR FEW SHALL SHARE THIS SACRED BOND
WHERE THEY DO SELDOM PART
AND IF BY CHANCE, YOU MEET THIS ONE
WHO SHARES YOUR EVERY DREAM
HOLD IT TIGHT AND CHERISH IT
IT MAY END BEFORE YOU DEEM

GRATEFUL...

YOU CAME INTO MY BITTER WORLD
WHERE THINGS WERE OFTEN BAD
YOU BROUGHT A LOT OF HAPPINESS
TO TIMES THAT HAVE BEEN SAD
YOU STOOD BY ME, IN TIMES OF NEED
NO MATTER WHAT WAS THOUGHT
AND GAVE YOUR LOVE SO FREELY
EVEN WHEN WE FOUGHT
IN YOU, I FOUND A GENTLE MAN
WHOSE FAULTS ARE VERY FEW
AND THOUGH I KEEP MY SECRETS DEEP
MY HEART BELONGS TO YOU

THANKS...

AS I RISE TO GREET THE SUN
THAT DRIES THE MORNING DEW
AS I BID THE MOON GOOD DAY
I THANK THE GODS FOR YOU
AS I GO INTO THE WORLD
THAT'S FILLED WITH SO MUCH HATE
I HAVE TO FALL ON BENDED KNEE
FOR LOVING YOU IS FATE
AS I WISH UPON A STAR
IN A SKY OF SPARKLING BLUE
AS I LOOK INTO YOUR EYES
I THANK THE GODS FOR YOU
AS ALL THE WATERS RIPPLE
IN ALL THE OCEANS DEEP
AS I HOLD YOU IN MY ARMS
MY HEART IS YOURS TO KEEP
AS WE TRAVEL ALONG ONE ROAD
WHERE THERE ONCE WAS TWO
AS WE SHARE OUR FONDEST DREAMS
I THANK THE GODS FOR YOU

ABANDONED...

MY LIFE HAS JUST BEEN SHATTERED
BEFORE MY VERY EYES
FOR ALL THAT I HAVE LIVED WITH
HAS BEEN SOME BITTER LIES
MY MOTHER SAID SHE LOVED ME
AND LEFT ME ON MY OWN
MY FATHER SAID HE'D HELP ME
WHERE HE WAS, WAS NEVER KNOWN
ALL ALONE – ABANDONED
WITH SOME FAMILY OR A FRIEND
PUSHED ASIDE – FORGOTTEN
THE PAIN, WILL IT EVER END
AND HOW DO I FORGIVE THEM
GO ON TO JUST BE FREE
HOW DO I FORGET THE SCARS
THAT MAKE UP ALL OF ME
AND WHERE DO I GO ON FROM HERE
WILL I LIVE TO DO THE SAME
WILL I BREAK A CHILD'S HEART
AND IN HIS EYES, SEE SHAME
SACRIFICED FOR SELFISHNESS
IN MY TIME OF DIRE NEED
LOST WITHIN THE DARKNESS
AND A HEART SO FULL OF GREED
ALL ALONE – ABANDONED
NO ONE THERE TO CLING UNTO
PUSHED ASIDE – FORGOTTEN
I WOULDN'T WISH THIS, EVEN ON YOU

YOUR EVERYTHING...

I WANT TO BE EVERYTHING TO YOU
THE RAIN, THE SNOW, THE SUNSHINE TOO
I WANT TO BE WITHIN YOUR HEART
WHEN WE'RE TOGETHER OR APART

I WANT TO BE YOUR EYES AND EARS
THE ONE WHO CRIES, THE ONE WHO CHEERS
I WANT TO BE IN ALL YOUR DREAMS
THE ONE WHO COOKS, THE ONE WHO CLEANS

I WANT TO BE THE ONE YOU LOVE
THE ONE WHO'LL TAKE THE PUSH AND SHOVE
I WANT TO BE WITHIN YOUR LIFE
AS YOUR PARTNER AND AS YOUR WIFE

REVISED FROM MARCH 21, 1987 (AGE 19)

WALK AWAY...

I NEVER THOUGHT I'D SEE THE DAY
WHEN ALL GOOD THINGS SHOULD END
OUR LOVE IS GONE AND NOW I FEAR
THAT WE CANNOT BE FRIENDS
BUT TAKE TO HEART, THERE WAS A TIME
WHEN I DEEPLY CARED
THINK ABOUT THE THINGS WE'VE DONE
AND ALL THOSE THINGS WE'VE SHARED
BUT, NOW IT'S TIME TO TURN AROUND
AND WALK THE OTHER WAY
I LOVED YOU ONCE, SO VERY MUCH
TOO MUCH TO BEG YOU STAY
I'LL THINK OF YOU IN TIMES TO COME
AND IN ALL MY NIGHTLY DREAMS
I'LL THINK ABOUT THE LIFE WE SHARED
WHICH WAS BETTER THAN IT SEEMS

REVISED FROM MAY 15, 1987 (AGE 19)

LOST HOPE

REALITY...

WE ARE THE PEOPLE
WHO LIVE OFF THE LAND
WE HOLD OUR OPPONENTS
IN THE PALMS OF OUR HANDS
WE LOOK WITH OUR EYES
WHILE THEY SEE WITH THEIR HEARTS
WE LIVE FOR THE LIGHT
AND FEAR FOR THE DARK
WE SEE THINGS STRANGE
WE HEAR THINGS WILD
WE FEAR THE ABSURD
AND PROTECT THE CHILD
WE TURN ON THE WEAK
WE RUN FROM THE STRONG
WE LAUGH AT THE LIES
WHILE THEY SING OUR SONG
THEY CALL US THE DREAMERS
WHILE WE WAIT FOR THE END
THEY CALL US THE LIARS
FOR PROTECTING OUR FRIENDS
WE GIVE OUR COMPLAINTS
HE LENDS US HIS EARS
YET, WE STAND ALL ALONE
IN OUR RIVER OF TEARS

SMALL & FRAIL...

I'M LIKE A CHILD
WHO IS TRAPPED BEHIND
A WALL ...... NOT STRONG ENOUGH
TO MOVE IT
AND NOT
BRAVE ENOUGH TO TRY

ALONE...

ALONE, FULL OF SHAME
AND NOWHERE TO TURN
THE SKIES ARE SILENT
BUT THE SUN STILL BURNS
ALONE AND UNHAPPY
MY EYES FULL OF TEARS
TOMORROWS ARRIVED
AND MY FUTURES NOT CLEAR
ALONE AND LONELY
I'M APART FROM MY FRIENDS
TODAYS ONLY MEMORIES
WILL LEAD TO THE END
ALONE AND AFRAID
I TURN FROM THE NIGHT
SMALL CREATURES ARE CALM
AND THE MOON IS SO BRIGHT
I'M FRIGHTENED HERE
AND MY FUTURES UNKNOWN
BUT I MUST REMAIN
SILENT... AND... ALONE

DEPRESSION...

I GET THIS URGE
AND I'M ABOUT TO CRY
A LONELY FEELING
AND I DON'T KNOW WHY
MY STOMACH GOES CRAZY
FROM BUTTERFLIES TO KNOTS
ONE SECOND I'M COLD
ANOTHER I'M HOT
I SPEND SLEEPLESS NIGHTS
WITH TIRED DAYS
TO LOOK FOR AN ANSWER
AND SOME OTHER WAY
I'M LOSING THE BATTLE
THERE'S NO WAY TO WIN
A HORRIBLE FEELING
AS DEPRESSION SETS IN

SHATTERED...

IF YOU WANT ME, I'LL BE IN THE DARKEST
CORNER OF THE WORLD – HIDING.
HIDING FROM ALL
- SHATTERED -
I LOOK ONLY TO SEE A SHATTERED IMAGE.
ONE MADE OF TENDERNESS AND VIOLENCE.
I HAVE NEVER SEEN THIS IMAGE BEFORE
NOR HAVE I EVER FELT SO STRANGELY. I
KNOW WHO IT IS; I GUESS I'VE ALWAYS
KNOWN. IT'S MY IMAGE TORN BETWEEN LOVE
AND HATRED, REALITY AND FANTASY. WHAT
I WOULD GIVE TO BE A MIRRORED
REFLECTION – WHOLE AND UNBROKEN.
UNHARMED BY MANS WAYS. BUT NO! NO
GLUE WILL EVER MAKE ME THE ONE PIECE I
WAS BEFORE. NO ONE CAN BREAK THE WEBS
THAT HAVE MADE EVERYTHING
UNBALANCED IN MY LIFE.

OUTCASTS...

WE ARE THE OUTCASTS
FROM A WORLD NOW PAST
THE TRUTH SHALL CONQUER
BUT HOW LONG WILL IT LAST
THERE'S WAR WITH DECEPTION
DECEPTION WITH LIES
SEX WITHOUT LOVERS
AND LOVE WITHOUT TIES
THERE'S SCHOOLS WITHOUT STUDENTS
KIDS WITHOUT HOMES
PARENTS WITHOUT SPOUSES
AND WE STAND ALONE
WE LIVE IN A TIME
WHERE NO MAN SURVIVES
WE'RE THE UNLUCKY
WE REMAIN ALIVE

WAR & PEACE...

I KNOW WHAT I NEED TO
BELIEVE WHAT I MUST
I FIND TRUTH IN THE ANSWERS
BUT IN NO ONE I TRUST
I LIVE FOR THE FUTURE
BUT FORGET NOT THE PAST
I THINK OF THE WARS
AND THE PEACE THAT WON'T LAST

FEARS...

SOMETIMES I FEEL LIKE THE WHOLE WORLD IS CLOSING IN ON ME AND I DON'T KNOW WHO I AM. ALL I WANT TO DO IS RUN AS FAR AWAY AS POSSIBLE. BUT IF I DO, I'LL BE LIKE SO MANY OTHERS. THEY SAY THE ONLY THING TO FEAR IS FEAR ITSELF AND THAT'S ENOUGH FOR ME. IF I COULD FACE IT AND LET IT GO, THINGS WOULD BE FINE. YET, IT'S EASIER TO SAY THAN DO. SO FOR NOW, I'LL KEEP RUNNING UNTIL THERE IS NOWHERE LEFT AND I'LL KEEP BEING SOMEONE ELSE UNTIL I FIGURE OUT WHO IT IS I'M SUPPOSE TO BE.

GONE...

I SAT BESIDE THE SHORELINE
AND WATCHED THE WATER FLOW
I LISTENED TO THE ANIMALS
AND FELT MY SPIRITS GROW

HERE, THIS CLOSE TO NATURE
YOU THINK ALL THINGS ARE RIGHT
THEN AT HOME, WITH TVS ON
OUR BODIES CRY IN FRIGHT

WHERE HAS THIS WORLD GONE,
WHEN EVERYONE WAS FREE?
I DIDN'T HAVE TO LOCK THE DOORS
OR BE ANYONE ELSE, BUT ME

REPETITION...

      EACH DAY IS LIKE A THOUSAND YEARS. ALL SEEM TO RUN THE SAME. THEY BECOME WEEKS, THEN MONTHS, THEN THEY BECOME YEARS. NOTHING IS EVER DIFFERENT. THE BEGINNINGS ARE HARD TO RECALL, THE ENDS ARE LONGED FOR AND WE ARE LOST SOMEWHERE BETWEEN.

FOREVER...

EACH DAY IS A FOREVER. A NEVER ENDING MOMENT. SLOW AND OFTEN PAINFUL TO FILL THE VOIDS IN LIFE. MOST RUN THE SAME. SOME FILLED THE TEARS. EACH MORNING FORGOTTEN, EACH NIGHT A LIFETIME, SOMETHING WE LONG TO END.

SORROW...

LIKE BLACKENED WATERS
IN FORESTS DEEP
SADNESS LINGERS
LIKE RAIN I WEEP
MY SORROW CLOUDS
ANY LIGHT THERE BE
AM I ALONE
LIKE THE WILLOW TREE
CAN I REACH
TO CARESS THE SKY
TO FEEL IT'S WARMTH
OH NO! NOT I
MY DESTINY STANDS
WITH BRANCHES LOW
MY HEART A WOUND
NO LOVE TO GROW

LIFE...

BOREDOM, SADNESS
TEENAGE FEARS
LOVE AND LAUGHTER
HEARTBREAKS, TEARS

EACH DAY WE LIVE
AND SUFFER MORE
EACH NIGHT WE HIDE
BEHIND CLOSED DOORS

REGRETS...

EACH DAY IS
A NEW BEGINNING
TO A LIFE
I'D LIKE TO END
EACH MOMENT
A CONSTANT BATTLE
BETWEEN A LOVER
OR A FRIEND
EACH MORNING HAS
IT'S SILENT HOPE
FOR ALL
THE YET TO BE'S
EACH EVENING HOLDS
THE BITTER FEAR
OF THOSE
I'LL NEVER PLEASE

LOST HOPE...

I HAVE NOTHING LEFT TO BELIEVE IN
IT'S ALL BEEN WIPED AWAY
LIKE SAND ON A BEACH, ON A RAINY NIGHT
NO STARS TO GUIDE MY WAY
THERE'S A RIVER ALL AROUND ME
NO LAND TO SET FOOT ON
ALL MY DREAMS HAVE BURNED TO ASHES
AND THE FIRE BLAZES ON
I'M THE ONLY ONE THAT'S OUT HERE
THERE'S NO OTHER SOUL AROUND
THEY'RE ALWAYS SOMEWHERE ELSE
ON SAFE AND STURDY GROUND
I'D GIVE MY LIFE, TO CHANGE IT ALL
AND MAKE IT ALL BE RIGHT
TO LIVE & LOVE AND HOPE & DREAM
AND FEEL SAFE WHEN I SLEEP AT NIGHT

NOTHING LEFT...

POISON IN THE HEARTS AND MINDS
OF ALL OF THOSE WHO LIVE
HATRED, FEAR AND RACISM
IS ALL THERE IS LEFT TO GIVE
THERE'S NO MORE LOVE, IN ALL THE WORLD
NO MORE JOY IN LIFE
THERE'S NO MORE HOPE FOR BETTER DAYS
FOR THE MOTHER OR THE WIFE
THERE'S NO MORE GOLDEN RAINBOWS
NOTHING LEFT TO DREAM
NO MORE TRUST IN ALL MANKIND
JUST LIES AND BITTER SCHEMES

FIGHTS...

I'M SCARED OF LOSING SANITY
AND ALL THOSE THINGS SO DEAR
LIFE HAS CRUMBLED BEFORE MY EYES
THERE'S NOTHING LEFT BUT TEARS

I TRY TO DO THE LITTLE THINGS
I THINK WILL MAKE HIM GLAD
BUT NO MATTER WHAT THE JOB I DO
HE ALWAYS ENDS UP MAD

HE CALLS ME NAMES AND BELITTLES ME
AND I FEEL SO SMALL INSIDE
HE GRABS & TWISTS AND WOUNDS MY HEART
TILL I WISH I WOULD HAVE DIED

NOTHING I SAY OR EVER DO
WILL EVER BE JUST RIGHT
SO, I'LL GRIT MY TEETH AND TRY AGAIN
AND WAIT FOR OUR NEXT FIGHT

THE COST...

WHAT IS THE COST
TO GIVE OUR HEART
TO SOMEONE THAT WE LOVE
IS IT BLOOD, OUR LIFE
OUR FAMILY
A SENTENCE TO HELL OR ABOVE
AN ARM, A LEG,
THE AIR WE BREATHE
OR JUST OUR FANTASIES
WHAT IS REALLY
THE COST WE PAY
FOR THOSE WE TRY TO PLEASE

CHOICES...

I'VE GOT ALL THESE FEELINGS
RUNNING AROUND INSIDE
MOST, I CAN'T EXPLAIN
I HAVE ALL OF THESE FEARS
HOLDING ONTO MY HEART
JUST LIKE A BALL & CHAIN
THERE'S NO MORE HAPPINESS
IN DAYS ARRIVING
AND NO MORE JOY IN SIGHT
THERE'S NO MORE LOVE
IN ALL THE WORLD
JUST THE LONELINESS OF THE NIGHT
THERE'S NO MORE HOPE
WHISPERED ON THE WIND
THROUGH THE BRANCHES OF A TREE
THERE'S NO MORE DREAMS
FOR THE YOUNGER ONES
AND NOTHING MORE TO SEE
THERE'S NO MORE ROOM
IN EITHER LIFE
WHAT WE ONCE HAD IS DEAD
THERE'S NO MORE DAYS
OF HANGING ON
AND NOTHINGS LEFT UNSAID
YET, HERE WE ARE
ALL ALONE – TOGETHER
FAKING IT DAY BY DAY
WE'VE LOST ALL HOPE
ON A BETTER LIFE
SO IT'S HERE, WE CHOSE TO STAY

YESTERDAY...

JUST A MOMENT IN TIME – A SIMPLE SNAP
OF THE FINGER. HERE AND THEN GONE AGAIN LIKE A LIGHTNING BOLT.
YET WE
SPEND SO MUCH OF OUR LIVES
PLANNING AND THINKING OF THE FUTURE
THAT WE FORGET WHAT'S IMPORTANT –
THE TODAY! AND WE'RE LEFT FEELING
LOST AND UNCERTAIN AS THE PRESENT
BECOMES THE PAST ANOTHER
YESTERDAY

TEARS AND SORROW...

T HE
E XPRESSION OF
A GGRAVATION
R AGE OR
S ADNESS

S OLITARY
O BSCURE
R ESTLESSNESS
R ESENTFULNESS
O VERWHELMING
W OE

DISENCHANTED...

WHEN I WAS BUT A LITTLE GIRL
LIFE SEEMED SO FULL OF CHARM
YET NOW THAT I AM OLDER
I CAN SEE THERE'S ONLY HARM
THE WORLD WAS FULL OF WONDER
AND LOTS OF THINGS TO DO
NOW IT'S ALL COLLAPSING
AND THE SKY IS HARDLY BLUE
THE RAIN IS OFTEN ACID
THE GROUNDS JUST OPEN UP
WHOLE CITIES ARE PULLED UNDER
LIKE SUGAR IN A CUP
PEOPLE USED TO LEAVE THEIR HOMES
CAREFREE, WITHOUT A DOUBT
NOW IT'S NOT WISE, TO BE ALONE
TO GO AND RUN ABOUT
I USED TO BE SO ENCHANTED
WITH ALL THE THINGS UNKNOWN
NOW I'M JUST DISAPPOINTED
AT ALL THE THINGS I'M SHOWN

FAILURE...

SOMETIMES LIFE DOESN'T TURN OUT
THE WAY YOU WANT IT TO
SOMETIMES THE COLORS OF A RAINBOW
ARE OFF A SHADE OR TWO
SOMETIMES THINGS THAT MADE YOU HAPPY
HAVE NO EFFECT AT ALL
SOMETIMES YOU THINK YOU'VE HAD ENOUGH
AND YOU'RE ABOUT TO FALL

DAYS AWAKENING...

IN BETWEEN THE HOURS
WHEN DUSK GIVES BIRTH TO DAWN
A HEART WILL FALL IN SILENCE
YET ANOTHER WILL LINGER ON
AND IN THIS DAYS AWAKENING
THERE'LL BE NO LOVE TO GAIN
FOR FEAR AND ALL ITS HATRED
WILL BE THE KING IN REIGN
THERE'LL BE NO JOYOUS DESTINY
FOR SOULS IN GREAT DESPAIR
THERE'LL BE NO GENTLE – GUIDING HAND
FOR MINDS THAT NEED REPAIR

ALONE...

I HAD A DREAM
AND IT CAME TRUE
I THOUGHT OF LOVE
AND THEN, I FOUND YOU
I HID MY HEART
TO YOU, I LIED
TO KEEP ME SAFE
NO TEARS I CRIED
YOU SAVED MY LIFE
I CAN NOT DENY
BUT TO BE YOUR BLOSSOM
THIS ROSE WOULD DIE
FOR I WAS MEANT
TO BE ALONE
TO SURVIVE THIS WORLD
ALL ON MY OWN

FAMILIES

FRIENDS...

A FRIEND
IS SOMEONE WHO
YOU CAN TRUST WITH ALL YOUR
SECRETS, NO MATTER HOW LARGE THEY
MAY BE

OVERDOSE...

HERE THEY STAND, IN HIS RIVER OF BLOOD
WAITING FOR THE END
SINGING SADLY, SCREAMING MADLY
WHO ARE THEY GONNA SEND
PEOPLE WERE SMOKIN', CHILDREN WERE TOKIN'
KILLING THEIR INNER SELF
GOING CRAZY, GETTING LAZY
PULLING DOWN THE SHELF
NOW HERE HE LIES, IN A BED OF SATIN
LOOKING AT THE NIGHT
FATHERS SIGHING, MOTHERS CRYING
AND THE CHILDREN ARE FILLED WITH FRIGHT
AN OVERDOSE OF CHINA WHITE
AND A LITTLE MARY JANE
THE BOY LIVES IN A DEAFENING SILENCE
AND, BY HIMSELF WAS SLAIN

MY CHILD...

EACH DAY MY BELLY
AND BREASTS WILL GROW
TO RELEASE A CHILD
THAT'S FRIEND AND FOE
A CHILD I'LL RAISE
ON HOPE AND LOVE
AND ONE I'LL TEACH
OF THE LORD ABOVE
YET WHEN I THINK
IT BRINGS ME WOE
THEY HAVE A FATHER
THEY'LL NEVER KNOW
BUT THAT DOESN'T SEEM
SO VERY BAD
CAUSE HE GAVE ME SOMETHING
I'VE NEVER HAD
AND EVEN THOUGH
I WAS NAUGHTY AND WILD
I'LL DO MY BEST TO RAISE
A HAPPY AND HEALTHY CHILD

THE CHILD...

THE CHILD
WHICH GROWS
WITHIN MY WOMB
WAS CONCEIVED IN PASSION
BUT WILL BE RAISED
WITH LOVE UNTOLD

MADE OF CHILD...

WHY CAN'T THIS WORLD
BE MADE OF CHILD
WHY CAN'T IT BE YOUNG
AND FREE AND WILD
WHY CAN'T IT BE GENTLE
AND FREE TO LOVE
NO BLACK OR WHITE
NO PUSH OR SHOVE
WHY CAN'T IT BE BRAVE
AND FREE OF FEAR
TO LIVE AMONG LOVE
AND SONG AND CHEER
WHY CAN'T IT BE INNOCENT
TO KNOW TRUTH AND NOT LIES
WHY CAN'T IT BE STRONG
TO GROW OLD AND SO WISE
HOW CAN WE TURN BACK
TO ONCE WHEN WE SMILED
RETURN TO THOSE DAYS
AND A WORLD MADE OF CHILD

TWO SIDES...

SHOW ME TO AN HONEST MAN
AND I'LL PROVE TO YOU HE LIES
SHOW ME TO A COLLEGE BOY
AND I'LL PROVE THE BEGGARS WISE
SHOW ME TO A FAITHFUL WIFE
I'LL SHOW YOU SHE WILL CHEAT
SHOW ME TO A BULLY CHILD
I'LL PROVE THAT HE'S BEEN BEAT
SHOW ME TO A BASTARD SON
I'LL PROVE HOW MUCH HE'S LOVED
SHOW ME TO THE STRONGEST MAN
I'LL PROVE HE CAN BE SHOVED
SHOW ME TO A LIARS WORLD
I'LL SHOW YOU WHERE THERE'S HATE
SHOW ME TO A LONELY GIRL
I'LL PROVE SHE HAS A MATE
SHOW ME TO AN EMPTY ROOM
I'LL SHOW YOU WHERE TO HIDE
SHOW ME TO A FLATTENED COIN
I'LL PROVE IT HAS TWO SIDES

GOD'S GIFT...

I WAS NOT GIVEN A FANCY HOUSE
WITH MAIDS FROM ROOM TO HALL
I DID NOT HAVE THE DIAMONDS AND GOLD
OR VERY MUCH AT ALL
I WAS NOT GIVEN FLASHY CLOTHES
OF SATIN OR COSTLY SILK
I DIDN'T DRINK THE FINE CHAMPAGNES
CAUSE ALL WE HAD WAS MILK
BUT I WAS GIVEN SPECIAL GIFTS
I NEVER CAN REPAY
THE LAND, THE SKY AND THE OCEAN
ON WHICH I GROW AND PLAY
I WAS GIVEN EYES TO SEE
GOD'S BEAUTY ALL AROUND
I WAS GIVEN EARS TO HEAR
ALL HIS HEAVENLY SOUNDS
I WAS GIVEN A NOSE TO SMELL
THE FLOWERS IN THE AIR
I WAS GIVEN A MOUTH TO TASTE
THOSE THINGS FOR WHICH I CARE
I WAS GIVEN A HEART TO LOVE
AND KEEP THINGS SAFE FROM HARM
THE FINAL GIFT FROM GOD TO ME
WAS TO KNOW THE SERPENTS CHARM

I AM – ME...

WHY IS EVERYONE SO UNSATISFIED
WITH WHO I'VE GROWN TO BE
I'M NOT A THIEF OR MURDERER
I'M JUST A SIMPLE – ME
I'M NOT SOMEONE WHO'LL TELL A LIE
TO BRING YOU TO MY SIDE
I'M NOT SOMEONE WHO'LL SLAM THE DOOR
AND LET YOU FREEZE OUTSIDE
I'M NOT SOMEONE WHO'LL RISK A LIFE
JUST TO SAVE MY OWN
I'M SELDOM CRUEL TO ANIMALS
IT'S THEIR LAND ON WHICH I'VE GROWN
I'M NOT A WOLF IN CLOTHES OF SHEEP
OR THE DEVIL IN DISGUISE
I'M NEITHER BLIND OR STUPID
I'M ALSO NOT ALL WISE
I'M JUST SOMEONE WHOSE HAD IT ROUGH
BUT STILL HAS HOPES AND FEARS
SOMEONE WHO LAUGHS AT COMEDIES
AND WHO'LL BE THE FIRST TO CHEER
I'M SOMEONE WHOSE HEART'S BEEN BROKEN
IN MORE WAYS THAN I CAN SAY
SOMEONE WHOSE DREAMS OF TOMORROW
ARE BETTER THAN TODAY
SO PLEASE DON'T MISTRUST OR JUDGE ME
UNTIL ALL THE FACTS ARE KNOWN
YOU'LL LIKE THE PERSON I'VE BECOME
FOR IT'S INTO – ME, I'VE GROWN

COMMON THREADS...

IN ALL OF OUR LIVES
WHETHER WE'RE YOUNG OR OLD
WE ALL HAVE LITTLE PROBLEMS
AND SIMILAR STORIES TOLD
EVERYONE HAS BAD DAYS
WE'RE SURE WE CAN'T SURVIVE
PRECIOUS TENDER MOMENTS
WHEN WE'RE GLAD TO BE ALIVE
ALL OF US HAVE DREAMS IN LIFE
WE CHOOSE TO NOT FORGET
PEOPLE WE KNEW OR CARED ABOUT
WE RATHER WOULD NOT HAVE MET
WE'VE WISHES MADE ON FALLEN STARS
WE WOULD LIKE TO HAVE ERASED
FEARS WE RAN AWAY FROM
WE SHOULD HAVE STAYED AND FACED
WE'VE JOYS OF CHILDREN BEING BORN
TO THOSE WE HOLD SO DEAR
AND TEARS WE'VE SHED IN SADNESS
FOR LOVED ONES NO LONGER HERE
IT'S ALL THESE THINGS THAT BIND US
TO A WORLD THAT'S OURS TO SHARE
COMMON THREADS OF LIVING
WHERE WE MUST LEARN TO CARE

A LITTLE GOOD...

BENEATH THE WINGS OF TRAGEDY
WHERE DARKNESS ALWAYS FALLS
WITHIN THE HOMES AND FAMILIES
YOU'LL FIND HEARTS WITH CONCRETE WALLS
WHERE EVIL SPINS ITS UGLY WEB
A LITTLE GOOD IS DONE
AND WITH SAD PASSING OF ELDER SOULS
A PRECIOUS NEW BABE SHALL COME

VIOLENCE...

LAYING IN A COLD DARK ALLEY
CLOTHING TORN TO SHREDS
RAPED AND BEATEN BRUTALLY
ANOTHER VENGEANCE FED
HIDING IN A CORNER ROOM
BONES BRUISED AND SLIGHTLY BROKEN
YOUR HUSBAND SOBERS UP A BIT
A SINGLE THOUGHT IS SPOKEN
A CHILD'S KILLED IN IGNORANCE
BY A ROBBER WITH A GUN
ANOTHER'S BORN ON CRACK-COCAINE
AND ONE DECIDES TO RUN
PEOPLE LIVING ON THE STREETS
WITH NOT A HOME TO GO
FACELESS MURDERED BODIES
WITHOUT A NAME TO KNOW
IN ALL THE WORLD, WHAT'S COME TO BE
IS A RASH OF RUTHLESS VIOLENCE
AND IN THE LIGHT OF EARLY DAWN
IT'S ALL FORGOTTEN, IN THE SILENCE

ANGRY ONE...

SHE'S GOT HAIR OF FIRE
A HEART MADE OUT OF STONE
A VOICE LIKE THE THUNDER
AND A TOUCH TO CHILL YOUR BONES

SHE'S GOT THE EYES OF A DEMON
WORDS AS SHARP AS SPEARS
EVERYTHING YOU WHISPER
IS EVERYTHING SHE HEARS

SHE'S ONE MAN'S OBSESSION
AND ANOTHER MAN'S DREAM
SHE'LL DRIVE YOU ALL CRAZY
CAUSE SHE IS NOT WHAT SHE SEEMS

FAMILIES...

M AGNIFICENTLY
O PTIMISTIC
T HANKFUL
H ELPFUL
E NERGETIC
R ESOURCEFUL
S UPPORTIVE

F ORGIVING
A DORING & ALWAYS
T EACHING
H ONEST &
E AGER
R ESPONSIBLE
S PECIAL

C HAOTIC YET
H APPY, VERY
I MAGINATIVE &
L OVING. ALWAYS
D ARING &
R EBELLIOUS
E NERGETIC &
N UTTY

COPS...

I HEAR THEM ALL SCREAMING
THROUGH THE DARKNESS OF NIGHT
THEIR SIRENS ALL BLARING
NOTHING SEEMS TO BE RIGHT
CREEPING THROUGH THE SHADOWS
SO AS THEY WON'T BE SEEN
BRING THEM IN, PAT EM' DOWN
ENSURE EACH ONE IS CLEAN
THEY DON'T WANT TO CHASE YOU,
IN A HEARTBEAT THEY WILL!
TAKE AIM WITH THE KNOWLEDGE
THEY WILL SHOOT YOU – TO KILL!
EACH OF THEM KNOWS THE STREETS
MOST COULD WALK THEM ALL – BLIND
THEY TAKE CALLS WITH PAPER,
KIDS, DOGS AND STUFF TO FIND
ARRESTING THE BAD GUYS
THEY LIVE LIFE ON THE LINE
ENTRUSTING EACH OTHER
CHECK, EVERYONE IS FINE
YOU PROBABLY KNOW ONE
OR MAYBE EVEN TWO
THE MEN WEARING BADGES
THE OFFICERS IN BLUE

NATURE

SNOW...

YOU FALL
WITH DIGNITY
LIKE SHATTERED CRYSTAL
COVERING THE EARTH WITH A SHIELD
OF WHITE

FOG...

THICKENED
AIR...A DARK CLOUD
OF HEAVY MIST GIVES
US THE FEELING THAT DEATHS PRESENT
HERE – NOW!

SUN...

YOU SEEM
TO COME AND GO
LIKE THE DAYS. LEAVING A
RAY OF BRIGHT COLORS TO LIGHTEN
OUR WAY

BIRD...

BLACK CROW
I WATCH YOU DANCE
WHILE YOU SEARCH FOR YOUR FOOD
IN THE MORNINGS GRASS THEN, AWAY
YOU FLY

CROW...

I WATCH
YOU PERCH ON THAT
TREE, LOOKING AT THE WORLD
AS IF YOU WERE THE KING AND IT
YOUR SLAVE

DEVIL IN THE SKY...

YOU SOAR
SENDING CHILLS AND
SHIVERS DOWN EACH ONES SPINE
SEARCHING FOR SOME FOOD TO CONSUME
TODAY

TREE...

GENTLY
SWAYING IN THE
WIND, YOU MAKE YOURSELF A
HOME FOR ALL CREATURES UNDER THE
SKY

FLOWER...

YOU DO
NOT MOVE OF YOUR
OWN FREE WILL, YET YOU ARE
ALIVE. SOMEDAY YOU WILL BLOSSOM
THEN, FADE

STAR LAKE, WISCONSIN...

THERE THEY SAT WITH BRIEF WINDS MAKING THE WATER CURL AND ROCK THE MAN FILLED BOAT, WHICH HAD BEEN RENTED EARLY YESTERDAY. THE AIR STILL UNTOUCHED BY MAN'S INVENTIONS GAVE THEM A FEELING OF PEACE AND TRANQUILITY.

PINE AND BIRCH TREES LINED THE OUTER EDGES OF THE LAKE WITH DIFFERENT SHADES OF GREEN. MANY OF THEM LYING ON THEIR SIDES IN ANGUISH AFTER A GREAT STORM HAD TAKEN AWAY THEIR LIFE.

THE CLOUDS SOFT AND COTTONY HUNG OVER THE LAKE IN A GRACEFUL MANNER, SHOWING ONLY A SMALL PORTION OF THE CRYSTAL BLUE SKY.

BIRDS NESTING IN THE ROCKS WERE SOON TO CAUSE OVERCAST AS A HAWK DESCENDED UPON THEM. THEN, CLIMBING BACK UP INTO THE SKY FILLING THE AIR WITH HIS CRY. PIERCING SHRIEKS THAT COULD STIR ANY SOUL.

FINALLY, THE SOUND OF A MOTOR FILLED THE AIR AS MAN AND HIS FAMILY HEADED FOR HOME AND REALITY.

BLESSED TEARS...
(A THUNDERSTORM)

TODAY THE GODS WERE ANGRY
THEIR VOICES FILLED THE SKY
THEY SCREAMED OF ALL THE SINNERS
AND THE WORLD THAT WE LET DIE

HEAVEN OPENED ITS PEARLY GATE
AND THERE WAS A FLASH OF LIGHT
THEN THE SKY WAS DARKENED
OUR WORLD BECAME AS NIGHT

ANGELS FELL ON BENDED KNEE
OUR HEARTS WERE FILLED WITH FEAR
THEN HEAVEN OPENED ONCE AGAIN
TO DROP THEIR BLESSED TEARS

WINTER...

I WALKED ALONG THE SHATTERED SHORE
WHERE THE SNOW BEGAN TO MELT
I GLANCED ACROSS THE WATERS DEEP
AND A PEACEFULNESS I FELT
THE SUN GLARED ACROSS THE ICE
LIKE A MIRROR IN THE SUN
THE CHILDREN IN THEIR WINTER CLOTHES
RAN SCREAMING IN SHEER FUN
THE TREES BENT DOWN SO HEAVILY
THEIR BRANCHES BRUSHED THE GROUND
THE WIND, IT BLEW SO BRISKLY
THAT IT MADE A CRACKLING SOUND
THESE TIMES NOW, ARE COLD AND BITTER
AND FOREVER THEY SEEM TO LAST
BUT, AS ALL THINGS IN NATURE
THIS TOO SHALL BECOME THE PAST
BIRDS WILL RETURN, FROM WARMER LANDS
AND JOYOUS SONGS THEY'LL BRING
GRASS WILL GROW AND FLOWERS BLOOM
AND WINTER WILL BOW DOWN – TO SPRING

AUTUMN MORNINGS...

IN A BLAZE OF BURNT UMBER
AND SUBTLE SHADES OF GRAY
A SILVERY BLUE HORIZON
THE LIGHT GIVES BIRTH TO DAY

THE MOON BACKS DOWN IN SILENCE
AND LEAVES THE NIGHTLY SKY
THE SUN RISES TO TAKE ITS PLACE
AND THE DEW BEGINS TO DRY

NOW AWAKE FROM SLUMBER
THE WORLD ALL FRESH AND NEW
WHITE CLOUDS OF COTTON CANDY
HANG ABOVE A SKY SO BLUE

MISC.

MY PRINCE...

MY PRINCE
WHOSE ARMOR IS AS BRIGHT
AS THE SUN, WHOSE SMILE
IS AS WIDE AS ALL
OCEANS COMBINED
WILL COME ONE DAY
AND NEVER LEAVE

WHISPERS...

WHISPERS IN THE DARK
PROTRUDING FROM THE LIGHT
VOICES IN MY HEAD
TELL ME WHO'S RIGHT
OPENING DOORS
IN THE BACK OF MY BRAIN
CLINKING KEYS
I'M GOING INSANE
THE VOICES TELL ME
WHICH WAY I'M TO TURN
THE EMPTY BOOKS
FROM WHICH I'M TO LEARN
THE STRANGERS KEEP TALKING
WHEN I'M ALL-ALONE
HAUNTING AND TAUNTING
EACH PART OF MY HOME
SCREAMING IN ANGER
IN THE DEAD OF THE NIGHT
THEN ROLLING IN LAUGHTER
IN THE MORNINGS LIGHT
THE CRIES I HEAR
COME FROM SOMEWHERE INSIDE
THEY KICK AND THEY SCREAM
THEN, THEY RUN AND HIDE
THE SOUNDS I HEAR
ARE NOT OF MY OWN
THE WHISPERS ARE STARTING
PLEASE... LEAVE ME ALONE

PRINCE...

YOU ARE
MY LIFE AND DREAMS
YOU SHINE ON ME LIKE A
SILVER STAR, MAKING IT EASY
TO LOVE

ANGEL...

I'M SITTING HERE IN LONELINESS
SPEAKING WITH THE TREES
THEIR LOVELY BRANCHES BILLOWING
BUT THEY DON'T SEEM TO ANSWER ME
THE GOLDEN SUN SETS SOFTLY
IN THE WESTERN SKY
THEN IT SLOWLY SHADES TO GRAY
AND I'LL NEVER KNOW JUST WHY
SOMEWHERE IN THAT DARKNESS
I HEARD THAT SAME OLD TREE
I SCREAMED AND YELLED IN SILENCE
THIS NIGHT IS KILLING ME
A LIGHT FELL DOWN FROM HEAVEN
LIKE A SECOND SUN
NOW MY DAY HAS ENDED
AND THE WAR HAS JUST BEEN WON
WALKING THROUGH THE VALLEY
WITH AN EVER GOLDEN LIGHT
MY WINGS SPREAD OUT BEHIND ME
AT LAST, I AM IN FLIGHT

HELL...

A PURPLE HAZE
AND A YELLOWY MIST
A REDDENED FACE
AND A BLOODY FIST
HELL'S FIRE
ROAMS THE LAND
THE CHILDS LOOSE
WITH A KNIFE IN HAND
THE MOTHERS DEAD
AND HER BLOOD IS DRAINED
THE EVIL HAS WON
BUT WHAT HAS BEEN GAINED
THE EARTH HAS OPENED
AND THE CREATURES SET FREE
WILL I BE NEXT?
OR WILL HE LET ME BE?
THE SERPENTS EYES
IN A TERRIFYING RAGE
IT'S THE END OF THE STORY
DON'T TURN THE PAGE

...cont'd

HELL CONT'D...

ALL IS LOST
BUT THE WAR IS NOT WON
THE DEVILS OUT
AND THE GOOD IS UNDONE
THE LORD WILL COME
FROM THE GOLDEN SKIES
HE'LL FIGHT THE FEAR
AND CHANGE THE LIES
EVIL WILL LOSE
AND THE LORD WILL WIN
HE'LL PROTECT THE PEOPLE
AND LIFT THEIR SIN
THE BOOK CAN BE OPENED
AND THE STORY NOW READ
THE EVIL HAS ENDED
NO MORE BLOOD WILL BE SHED

SUMMER VACATION...

SUMMER NOT ONLY BRINGS FLOWERS
AND SUNSHINE. IT ALSO BRINGS A
FREEDOM – A FREEDOM FROM
SOMETHING AS BINDING AS SCHOOL.
BUT LET US NOT FORGET, WE CAME
HERE TO LEARN ALL THAT'S
POSSIBLE. AND FOR NOW, WE LEAVE
IT ALL BEHIND TO PLAY WITHIN OUR
WORLD. YET, WE HOLD ON TO THE
HOPES THAT WE CAN ENLIGHTEN
SOMEONE'S FUTURE WITH ALL THAT
WE HAVE LEARNED IN THE PAST.

SALEM...

SOMEWHERE OUT IN SALEM'S LOT
IN A DARK AND GLOOMY FIELD
THE PRINCE OF DARKNESS STANDS ALONE
AND RAISES HIS FLESHY SHIELD
CREATURES RISE FROM DEPTHS BELOW
AS HE CONJURES UP A SPELL
HIS VIRGIN BRIDE ARRIVES IN TERROR
THEN DESCENDS TO HELL
FIRES RISE ABOVE THE FLOOR
AS THEY ENTER THE BLOOD – STAINED GATE
THE INNOCENCE OF THE VIRGIN BRIDE
IS LEFT IN THE HANDS OF FATE

SPRING BREAK...

BRILLIANT RAYS
ACROSS THE LAND
SALTY WATERS
ENGULF THE SAND

LIFELESS BODIES
SIDE BY SIDE
STRING BIKINIS
AWAITING HIGH – TIDE

BUILT UP GUYS
SWIMMING BY
PRETTY GIRLS
WITH HEAVY SIGHS

FUTURES...

I FEAR THE FUTURE
AND WHAT IT MAY HOLD
I FEAR THE SPRING
AND THE WINTER'S COLD
I FEAR THE EMPTINESS
I FEEL INSIDE
I HATE THE LIES
I'VE TOLD TO HIDE
I FEAR THE NIGHT
BECAUSE OF THE DAWN
I AWOKE ONE DAY
AND IT ALL WAS GONE
I LIVE ALONE
IN A WORLD I MADE
IN EVERY WAY
I GUESS I HAVE PAID
THE THINGS I'VE DONE
I'M SORRY FOR
I PROMISE YOU THIS
THEY'LL HAPPEN NO MORE

DRAGONS...

THE SUN DOTH FALL
BEHIND THE HILL
THE MOON DOTH CAST
AN EERIE CHILL
A WIZZARD CHANTS
AN EVIL SPELL
THE FIRES RISE
THE BEAST FROM HELL
WITH WINGS AS BLACK
AS WATERS DEEP
HIS TONGUE CAN PUT
THY SOULS TO SLEEP
A LION'S HEAD
A SERPENTS TAIL
AN EAGLE'S CLAWS
A FISH LIKE SCALE
THE DRAGON COMETH
TO KILL THY KNIGHT
HIS BREATH OF FIRE
TO SWORD OF LIGHT
SEALED IN CAVERNS
DEPTHS BELOW
TAMED BY TOUCH
A CRYSTAL GLOW

RAINBOWS...

IT HAS BEEN SAID THAT RAINBOWS ARE SEEN
ONLY AFTER A HEAVY STORM. BUT I'VE
SEEN THEM ON THE DARKEST OF NIGHTS.
A THING OF SUCH BEAUTY MAY BE SEEN
AT ANYTIME. EVEN ON THE CLEAREST OF
NIGHTS IN THE EYES OF THOSE YOU
LOVE. AND THE POT OF GOLD AT THE
END OF THOSE RAINBOWS CANNOT BUY
OR REPLACE WHAT IS FELT WHEN YOU
LIE IN EACH OTHERS ARMS. A TRUE
RAINBOW MAY LAST ONLY A MOMENT IN
TIME YET, THE ONES YOU FIND TOGETHER
CAN LAST TILL ALL OF TIME COMES TO
AN END.

FREEDOM...

I'VE HEARD IT SAID THAT WE ARE ALL
FREE TO COME AND GO AS WE PLEASE.
FREE TO MAKE OUR OWN DECISIONS
ABOUT OUR LIVES. BUT, THEY ARE
WRONG! AS CHILDREN, OUR PARENTS
TELL US WHEN AND WHAT TO EAT, HOW
TO TALK AND DRESS AND WHEN TO
SLEEP. AS TEENS, WE HAVE THE
TEACHERS, OUR PARENTS AND OUR
FRIENDS COAXING US TO DO THINGS. AS
ADULTS, WE HAVE OUR SPOUSES, OUR
BOSSES AND OUR FRIENDS TELLING US
WHAT TO DO. THE GOVERNMENT ALSO
MAKES RULES FOR US TO FOLLOW. SO,
WE ARE NEVER REALLY FREE TO DO ANYTHING.
THERE WILL ALWAYS BE CHAINS TO CARRY,
TIES THAT CANNOT BE BROKEN
AND BONDS THAT WILL BE WITH US FOREVER.

DREAMS...

DREAMS WILL COME
WITH COLORS BRIGHT
ON ANGEL'S WINGS
ON MOONLIT NIGHTS
DREAMS OF HOPE
AND TRUST AND LOVE
NOT TEARS OR FRIGHT
BUT HOLY DOVES
YET, DARKER DAYS
WILL COME FOR ALL
WHEN SKIES ARE GRAY
AND DEMONS CALL
TO BRING US DREAMS
OF ANGER AND HATE
WITH LUST NOT LOVE
AND A FIERY FATE
BUT, DON'T DESPAIR
WHEN EVILS CALL
THE ANGELS WILL COME
AND GUARD US ALL

RUN AWAY...

IF I COULD RUN AWAY FROM HERE
I'D RUN SO FAR AND FAST
AND ANY HEARTACHE I COULD FEEL
SURELY WOULDN'T LAST
BUT IF I WENT AWAY FROM HERE
WHAT WOULD BE THE COST
ALL THE PLANS AND DREAMS I'VE MADE
COMPLETELY WOULD BE LOST
CAUSE FOR ALL OF THE ANGER
AND RESENTMENT INSIDE
THERE'S NOT A SINGLE PLACE
FROM OUR LOVE, I CAN HIDE

RAPE IS...

R EVENGE OUT OF
A NGER, NOT
P LEASURE OR
E XCITEMENT

R EVENGE OUT OF
A NGER FOR
P ERSECUTION &
E XILE

R OUGHNESS DUE TO
A GGRAVATION
P UNISHMENT BY
E XTREME VIOLENCE

TRUST...

T OTAL
R ELAXATION
U NDERSTANDING &
S INCERITY
T OWARDS OTHERS

TRAGEDY...

TRAGEDY STRIKES
IN ALL OF OUR LIVES
THEN, NOTHING
IS EVER THE SAME
IN A FLASH
OF THE MOMENT
IT ALL CAN BE GONE
AND WE'RE THE ONES
LOSING THE GAME

TIME...

EACH DAY WE LIVE
AND HOPE FOR THE FUTURE
YET, THERE IS NEVER
ENOUGH TIME TO DO ALL
THE THINGS WE WANT
BUT IT SEEMS LIKE WE
HAVE ALL THE TIME IN
THE WORLD TO REGRET
WHAT WE HAVE AND
HAVE NOT DONE

KUTULU...

FEEL HIS RHYTHM BENEATH THE GROUND
HEAR HIS EERIE – AWFUL SOUND
KNOW HE DREAMS & LAYS IN WAIT
FOR ONE AND ALL TO UNSEAL THE GATE
AND SET HIM FREE THAT VERY HOUR
TO SHED HIS WRATH & FEED HIS POWER
HE'S NOT OF US OR LIVING THINGS
HE CARES NOT WHAT CHAOS HE BRINGS
HE IS THE BEAST, THE ANCIENT ONE
WITH HIM LOOSE, ALL GOODS UNDONE
THE DEVIL'S DOG, A DEMON SNAKE
BE CAREFUL AT THE CHARMS YOU MAKE
FROM A WORLD OF DARK, NOW PAST
HE WAITS IN SLUMBER, FOR LIFE AT LAST

DREAMS...

DREAMS ARE GRANTED TO THOSE WITH
THE STRENGTH AND COURAGE TO SURVIVE ITS REALITY. NOT TO THOSE
WHO SIT IDLY BY WAITING FOR THINGS TO
BE GIVEN TO THEM! FOR DREAMS ARE
OBTAINABLE! BUT ONLY BY THOSE WITH
THE HEART AND SOUL TO DO BATTLE
WITH THE NON-BELIEVERS AND TAKE
WHAT IS RIGHTFULLY OURS!

CHARMS...

LET ME DO THE BIDDINGS
FOR ALL THE ANCIENT ONES
THROUGH YOUR POWERS AND MY STRENGTH
LET ALL OUR WARS BE WON
GIVE ME CHARMS TO BRING YOU HERE
UNTO THIS EARTHLY STATE
GIVE ME SERVANTS, TO BECKON THEE
AND BRING FORTH OUR MASTERS FATE
LET ME KNOW THE SERPENTS CHARM
AND ALL HIS SECRETS DEEP
YET PROTECT ME FROM HIS FLAMING BREATH
THAT PUTS MORTAL SOULS TO SLEEP

ADAM & EVE...

THERE ONCE WAS A GARDEN OF EDEN
WHERE EVERYTHING GLOWED OF LIFE
AND IN IT WAS A MAN CALLED ADAM
WHO FROM HIM, GOD MADE A WIFE
EVE WAS A WOMAN OF BEAUTY
WITH A SMILE AS PURE AS GOLD
BUT EVE, SHE HAD A CURIOUS SIDE
AND SO THE STORY IS TOLD
INTO THE GARDEN, A SERPENT CAME
WITH A BODY DARK AND THICK
HE TOOK ADVANTAGE OF HER INNOCENCE
AND PLAYED AN EVIL TRICK
HE TEMPTED HER WITH LUSCIOUS FRUIT
GOD STRICTLY HAD FORBADE
SHE HELD THE FRUIT TO ADAM'S MOUTH
AND FOR THEIR TREACHERY PAID
THEN UNTO OUR WORLD HAD COME
THE WRATH OF GOD AND FEAR
AND TO OUR CHILDREN'S CHILDREN'S SON
WE ALL MUST SHED A TEAR

HOPES AND DREAMS...

OUR DREAMS ARE GRANTED PASSAGE
ON SPARROW'S WINGS IN FLIGHT
AND SWIFTNESS SOMETIMES COMES
WITH BUT A PASSING OF A NIGHT

THERE'S HOPE THAT'S ALWAYS GIVEN TO
THOSE LIVES WITH SUCH DESPAIR
AND NO CROSS IS EVER HANDED DOWN
THAT'S MORE THAN WE CAN BEAR

YET WE LIVE WITH SUCH REGRET
WE ALWAYS STRIVE FOR MORE
AND THOSE THINGS THAT MATTER MOST
WE TEND TO JUST IGNORE

DO IT...

LAY ME DOWN
DO IT EASY
DO IT RIGHT
MAKE LOVE TO ME
FROM THE MORNING
UNTIL NIGHT
DON'T TRY TO IMPRESS ME
CAUSE THAT AIN'T WHAT I NEED
I'VE GOT THIS RAGING HUNGER
AND ON YOU, I WANT TO FEED
DO IT RIGHT
TAKE ME DOWN
MAKE ME SCREAM
MAKE MY WORLD SPIN ROUND
DO IT EASY
DO IT TONIGHT
OH TOUCH ME THERE
GOD IT FEELS SO OUT OF SIGHT

HALLOWEEN...

TONIGHT IS THE NIGHT
OF ALL HALLOWS EVE
WHEN ALL GHOSTS AND GOBLINS
ARE GRANTED THEIR LEAVE
FROM THE MOMENT OF DARKNESS
TILL FIRST LIGHT OF DAY
THEY'LL SLIP THROUGH OUR WORLD
TO FROLIC AND PLAY
THEY'LL WALK ALONG SIDE US
WITHOUT ANY DISGUISE
AMONGST TRICK OR TREATERS
WHO WILL NOT BE THE WISE
THEY'LL SETTLE THEIR DEBTS
AND EVEN THE SCORE
SAY THEIR GOOD-BYES THEN,
THEY'LL BE HERE NO MORE

CRYSTAL AXE...

AS ALL THE LIGHTS GO OUT
YOU, AS THE AUDIENCE WILL RISE
A BRAND NEW BAND WILL OPEN
WITH A DEAFENING SWEET SURPRISE

THEY'LL START OUT AS A SOUND
AND THEY'LL END IT IN A SONG
YOU'LL WANT TO LISTEN TO THEM
THE ENTIRE EVENING LONG

YOU'LL HEAR THEIR GUITARS ECHO
AND THEIR DRUMMERS ROLL
YOU'LL HEAR THE FIDDLERS PLAYING
SOME GOOD OL' ROCK AND ROLL

SO COME HERE CLOSER TO US
NOW SIT DOWN AND RELAX
THE SOUNDS YOU WILL BE HEARING
ARE FROM THE CRYSTAL AXE

TIME...

AS I SIT HERE, I GROW OLDER
WHILE TIME JUST SEEMS TO STAND
THE MOUNTAINS RISE AND CRUMBLE
AND WATERS FLOOD THE LAND

THE SUNS A BALL OF FIRE
BUT WILL IT FADE AWAY
WILL IT WAIT, TILL I'M DEAD AND GONE
TO RISE ANOTHER DAY

TIME IS EVER LASTING
BUT THE WORLD WILL COME AND GO
WE WON'T LAST FOREVER
THAT'S SOMETHING WE ALL SHOULD KNOW

SO TAKE IT ALL, A DAY AT A TIME
AND LIVE IT WHILE YOU CAN
THEN WHEN IT'S OVER, DON'T LOOK BACK
CAUSE YOU CAN'T RELIVE IT AGAIN

CARDS

VALENTINE...

I SAY I LOVE YOU
IN THINGS I DO
I SHOW I CARE
BY HOLDING YOU
YET THIS ONLY COMES
BUT ONCE A YEAR
AND WHEN IT DOES
I'M FILLED WITH CHEER
INSTEAD OF DOING
AND SHOWING
I'D RATHER JUST SAY;
"PLEASE BE MINE,
THIS VALENTINES DAY"

VALENTINE...

TO THE ONE
THAT I HOLD DEAR
I'D LIKE YOU TO KNOW
THIS DAY OF THE YEAR
IT BRINGS ME GREAT JOY
AND PEACE OF MIND
TO KNOW THERE WAS LOVE
FOR US TO FIND
AND AT THIS TIME
I'D LIKE TO SAY
I'M SO GLAD YOU'RE MINE
THIS VALENTINES DAY

A CHRISTMAS WISH...

CHRISTMAS BRINGS
A HEART FELT JOY
TO BOYS AND GIRLS
A BRAND NEW TOY
IT BRINGS A WORLD
OF WINTER WHITE
A SILVER GLOW
IN THE MIDST OF NIGHT
IT BRINGS NEW DREAMS
FOR THE YEARS TO COME
AND OFTEN HOPE
FOR THE LONELY ONE
WE WISH YOUR CHRISTMAS
IS ALL THAT IT CAN BE
AND WE HOPE THAT LOVE
WILL DECORATE YOUR TREE

CHRISTMAS...

TO THE ONE
THAT I HOLD DEAR
I WISH TO TELL YOU
THIS DAY OF THE YEAR
I KNOW HOLIDAYS
ARE NOT ALWAYS BRIGHT
I HOPE IT WILL CHANGE
THIS CHRISTMAS NIGHT
I HOPE THIS DAY
IS SO FULL OF FUN
AND I HOPE THAT IT'S SPENT
WITH A VERY LOVED ONE

A BIRTHDAY WISH...

TO WHO'S BEST
IN EVERY WAY
I WISH YOU LAUGHTER
AND HAPPINESS
ON THIS BIRTHDAY

HAPPY BIRTHDAY

THE ONE...

I GAVE MY ENTIRE HEART TO YOU
WITHOUT A SINGLE DOUBT
NO OTHER MAN COULD HOLD ME
CAUSE YOU'RE WHAT LOVES ABOUT
THERE'S NOT A TRAGIC FEAR IN ME
OR ANY PAST REGRET
NO ONE ELSE COULD TAKE YOUR PLACE
SO YOU REALLY NEED NOT FRET
I HAVE CHOSE TO STAND BY YOU
FOREVER AT YOUR SIDE
WHETHER TIMES ARE GOOD OR BAD
MY LOVE I WILL NOT HIDE
FOR I HAVE FOUND THE ONLY MAN
I WANT OR NEED IN LIFE
YOU BRING ME JOY AND HAPPINESS
YOU'RE MY HUSBAND AND I AM YOUR WIFE

VALENTINE...

I KNOW THERE ARE THOSE MOMENTS
WHEN ALL WE DO IS FIGHT
AND NO MATTER WHAT THINGS I DO
NOTHING SEEMS JUST RIGHT
PRECIOUS WORDS THAT WE SHOULD SAY
ARE RARE AND VERY FEW
AND THOUGH THEY HAVE BUT LITTLE MEANING
THERE ARE THINGS I WISH YOU KNEW
LIKE THE LAUGHTER YOU SEEM TO BRING
WITH YOUR SIMPLE CHARMS
AND THE WARMTH I FEEL INSIDE
WHEN I'M HELD WITHIN YOUR ARMS
AND THOUGH NOTHING IS EVER CONSTANT
THE FACT TO ALWAYS BE TRUE
IS NO MATTER HOW GOOD OR BAD THINGS GET
MY HEART BELONGS TO YOU
AND IF I'M NOT ALWAYS AT MY BEST
KNOW, I DO TRY IN EVERY WAY
NOW I'D LIKE TO SAY, "I LOVE YOU
AND HAPPY VALENTINES DAY"

VALENTINE...

THERE ARE SO MANY THINGS
THAT I CAN'T EXPLAIN
LIKE JOY AND FEAR
OR HEARTACHES AND PAIN

BUT THERE IS ONE THING
FOR WHICH I'M QUITE SURE
I SO DEEPLY LOVE YOU
AND FOR THIS, THERE'S NO CURE

SO I'D LIKE TO TAKE
THIS ONE TIME TO SAY;
"I LOVE YOU SO MUCH,
HAPPY VALENTINES DAY

VALENTINE...

FRIENDS LIKE YOU ARE A RARITY
AND CAN'T BE GROWN ON TREES
THEY CAN'T BE PRUNED LIKE ROSES
BUT, THEY'RE JUST AS SURE TO PLEASE
THEY'RE NOT SO DARK & SECRETIVE
AS THOSE WE CHOOSE TO LOVE
THEY'RE NOT LIKE CLOUDS ON RAINY DAYS
THEY'RE MORE LIKE STARS ABOVE
FRIENDS LIKE YOU BRING SUNSHINE
IN ALL THE LITTLE WAYS
SO, I'M GLAD TO HAVE A FRIEND LIKE YOU
TO SHARE THIS SPECIAL DAY

HAPPY VALENTINES DAY!

IT CAN'T BE CHRISTMAS...

CHRISTMAS ISN'T CHRISTMAS
WITHOUT THE ICY BITTER COLD
AND HOW COULD IT BE CHRISTMAS
WITHOUT THE STORIES SANTA TOLD?
CHRISTMAS WOULDN'T BE CHRISTMAS
WITHOUT THE CRACKLING OF THE SNOW,
AND ALL THE DECORATIONS
AND THE PRETTY LIGHTS A GLOW
JUST HOW COULD IT BE CHRISTMAS
WITHOUT PRESENTS WRAPPED UP TIGHT,
THE HOLLYS AND THE MISTLETOE,
THE SMELL OF COOKING THROUGH THE NIGHT
THERE'S NO WAY IT COULD BE CHRISTMAS
CAUSE MY CHORES ARE JUST NOT DONE!
YOU'LL HAVE TO HOLD YOUR HORSES,
I HAVE SOME MORE ERRANDS TO RUN.
I JUST KNOW IT CAN'T BE CHRISTMAS,
I FORGOT THE BLOODY TREE!
I HOPE YOU KNOW I'M FOOLIN'
MERRY CHRISTMAS ... TO ALL OF YOU ... FROM ME!

WELCOME TO THE BEGINNING

ISBN 141203502-3

Made in the USA
Columbia, SC
28 August 2025